by Jacqueline Hanks

To my sister, Nancy—
who knows a lot about being a friend

Published by Willowisp Press, Inc.
10100 SBF Drive, Pinellas Park, Florida 34666

Copyright © 1991 by Willowisp Press, Inc.

Printed in the United States of America

10 9 8 7 6 5 4 3 2 1

ISBN 0-87406-531-3

Benjamin Bear was a small, fuzzy brown bear who lived in the teddy bear basket at the department store. He used to be a happy little bear. But these days he didn't smile very much. Benjamin was down in the dumps because he didn't have a real home with a little boy or girl.

At night, Benjamin dreamed of sleeping in a warm bed, snuggled into a soft pillow next to a new friend.

The bear basket at the store wasn't soft or snuggly. The bigger bears tossed and turned, bumping Benjamin from one end of the basket to the other. It made him very sad.

One day Benjamin grew tired of being sad. He knew he was too small to be noticed beside the bigger bears. So he made up his mind to find a better spot.

"I'll find a place in the store where there aren't any other bears," Benjamin decided. "Then a little boy or girl will pick me for sure. Soon I'll have my very own bed to sleep in."

He bounced down from the basket and set out to find the perfect place.

Benjamin wandered past puzzles, yo-yos, and kites until he came to the party supply section. He grabbed a crayon and a piece of paper and drew a big sign. When he finished, it said, "Party bear wants to make your party special."

Benjamin put a party hat on his head, hung the sign around his neck, and climbed into a colorful gift box.

When boys and girls walked by the party section the next day, he made silly faces and threw confetti. He even put on a pretty bow. But everyone bought napkins or paper plates. No one was looking for a little teddy bear.

At the end of Benjamin's busy day, he was sad and tired.

"Maybe I'll find a home tomorrow," he told himself as he settled down to sleep.

Party Bear
wants to make
your party special!

The gift box was small and hard and lonely. There was no one for Benjamin to snuggle against to keep warm. He finally rolled himself up in a piece of pink tissue paper.

The next morning, the little teddy bear felt stiff and his neck hurt. He decided to move to another part of the store.

Benjamin stopped walking when he came to a dollhouse display.

"This is the perfect place to find a friend," he said.

He used his crayon to draw a big sign that said, "Bear hugs inside."

He explored the rooms in the dollhouse. Then he sat down at the tiny piano and sang. He called "yoo-hoo" to the children through the tiny windows.

The little girls who walked by wanted dollhouse furniture. They weren't looking for a teddy bear.

That night, he snuggled into a soft pillow in a warm dollhouse bed. But he still wasn't happy. He still hadn't found a real home. And he realized that he missed the other bears. A small tear trickled down his cheek.

When the store opened the next day, Benjamin was sitting in a little, red toy sports car.

"Honk! Honk!" the horn sounded as he pushed the button. He waved to all the boys and girls who walked by.

Soon one of the boys began playing with the car.

"Oh, boy!" Benjamin thought. "He likes me. Maybe he'll take me home."

The little boy raced the car up and down the aisles. He swerved it around corners and made it zigzag between the bikes and wagons.

Benjamin held on to the steering wheel tightly. He had never moved so fast before. He was scared.

Zoom! The car sped past the candy counter and nearly crashed into a shopping cart. Then, suddenly, the car screeched to a stop. Benjamin looked up and saw that he was right in front of the teddy bear basket.

The little boy picked him up and placed him in the teddy bear basket. Benjamin was excited to see his friends again. He had really missed them.

Soon, the store closed and all the bears grew tired. Benjamin fell asleep with a big smile on his face.

He was awakened the next morning by a little girl.

"I love you, little bear," she said, grinning. "You look so happy that you make me happy, too. I'm taking you home to live with me."

"Wow, I have my very own home with a little girl," Benjamin thought. "And it's all because I made her happy."

Now that his wish had come true, Benjamin couldn't stop smiling.